In the Language of My Captor

# SHANE McCRAE

*Hi Lauren Koleszar! I hope you like it!*

—[signature]

*9-27-18*

**Wesleyan University Press**

MIDDLETOWN, CONNECTICUT

# IN THE LANGUAGE OF MY CAPTOR

# Wesleyan Poetry

Wesleyan University Press

Middletown CT 06459

www.wesleyan.edu/wespress

Manufactured in the United States of America

Designed by Quemadura

Typeset in DIN and Scala

This project is supported in part by an award
from the National Endowment for the Arts.

**ART WORKS.** | **National Endowment for the Arts** arts.gov

### Library of Congress Cataloging-in-Publication Data

Names: McCrae, Shane, 1975– author.

Title: In the language of my captor / Shane McCrae.

Description: Middletown, Connecticut : Wesleyan
University Press, [2017] | Series: Wesleyan poetry

Identifiers: LCCN 2016035696 (print) | LCCN 2016041724
(ebook) | ISBN 9780819577115 (cloth : alk. paper) |
ISBN 9780819577139 (ebook)

Classification: LCC PS3613.C385747 A6 2017 (print) |
LCC PS3613.C385747 (ebook) | DDC 811/.6—dc23

LC record available at https://lccn.loc.gov/2016035696

5 4 3

For my families

*You will feed yourself five thousand times.* —THYLIAS MOSS

# Contents

# 4

1

## His God

I am the keeper tells

Me the most popular exhibit

You might not think this cheers me but it does

I'm given many opportunities

I like especially to ask the groups

Led by fat white men     I am careful to

Never address the fat man but the group

*How has it come // To pass*

*that I'm on* this *side of the bars*

*And you're on* that *side*

And     *Who stands in your shoes*

*You or the people you resemble*

*they don't give me shoes //* I say

Gesturing toward a zoo employee

and I smile

Often the people do not answer me

Often the fat man squints     and says *It real-* // *ly makes you think*

Something like that     or *There*

*but for the grace of God*     / I tell the keeper they must be

The daughters and the sons of nearer gods


I tell him my gods had to stay behind

To watch my people     / He likes it when I talk like that

the truth is I don't know

The keeper     when he's drunk


Sometimes he says I'm lucky

To have been rescued from my gods

And I should thank the man who bought me

I used to laugh at him     but now I grieve


I think // His god is not a god like mine     / His god

Is not a mother     not a father

not a hunter     not a farmer

his     / God is a stranger


from no country he has seen

## Panopticon

The keeper put me in the cage     with the monkeys

Because I asked to be

Put in the cage with the monkeys

Most of the papers say the monkeys


must     // Remind me of my family

The liberal papers say the monkeys must

Remind me of my home

The papers don't ask me


some days // I tuck notes     explanations

Into soft monkey shits

and call white children to the bars

I warn the parents     / But still they let their children come


And that's my explanation     / I am

their honest mirror

I say     *Whether you're here*

*to see me     or to see the monkeys*


*You're here to see yourselves*

# Privacy

I tell the keeper I don't know

What he or any white man means

When he says *privacy*

Especially

In the phrase *In the privacy*

*Of one's own home*　/ I understand

he thinks he means a kind of

Militarized aloneness

If he would listen I would tell him

Privacy is impossible

If one's community is

Not bound by love

Instead I tell him where I'm from we

Have no such concept

If he thinks I am / Too wise

he won't speak honestly

And so I make an     / Effort to make

my language fit his

Idea of what I am

I find with him     and with his guests


Because I'm on display in

A cage with monkeys

I / Must speak and act

carefully to maintain     / His privacy


and // If he would listen I would tell him

Where privacy

Must be defended

There is no privacy


I have become an // Expert on the subject

But I have also learned

The keeper will not trust me     / To understand

even what he has taught me

# What Do You Know About Shame

Late very late long after

The many families and the lone white man

Who stayed long after

The families had gone had gone


Last night the keeper staggered to my cage / Weeping

he said his wife

Was leaving him

And he would never see his son


Again I said I did not understand

Why he would never see his son again

He said     he was ashamed

And his // Wife was ashamed


and she was going back to

Her     *people* was his word

and / Taking the child

I said I did not understand

Why he would never see his son again

Again     I said there would be no

Ocean between his son and him

No bars


Between / Him and the ocean

if there were an ocean

And I said *Surely I am making you*

*A wealthy man*


*you can // Afford to travel*

*can you not*

The keeper     stepped close to my cage

and snarled / *Your women     / Tramp through the jungle*


*with their tits out // What do you know about*

*shame*     and I shouted *You are drunk*

*Go home and be / Drunk with your family*

*While you still can*

He growled

and struck the bar between us

And stumbled back and fell

*How do you know a white man's really*     *hurt* I laughed


*He*     */ Stops crying*

# Privacy 2

I tell the keeper I don't know

What he or any white man means

When he says *privacy*

Especially

In the phrase *In the privacy*

*Of one's own home*     / I understand

he thinks he means a kind of

Militarized aloneness

If he would listen I would ask him whether

The power / To enforce alone-

ness and aloneness

can exist together

Instead I tell him where I'm from we

Have no such con-

cept if he thinks I am     / Too wise

he won't speak honestly

And so I talk the way the men

He says are men like me

Talk in the books he reads to me

I understand


Those books are not supposed to make me wise

And yet I think perhaps

They show me what he means

By *privacy*     // Perhaps


by *privacy* he means / This

certainty he has that

The weapons he has made

Will not be used against him

# In the Language

I *cannot* talk about the place I came from

I do not want it to exist

The way I knew it

In the language of my captor

The keeper asks me why I

Refuse him this

I think to anyone who came from / The place I came from

It would be obvious

but     // I did not think my people

Superior to other people     before

The keeper's language has infected me

I knew of     // Few people

Beyond the people / I knew

before and when I met new people

The first thing I assumed was

they were just like me

Perhaps even relatives

Who had before my birth been lost

In the jungle or on the plain

Or on the other side of the mountain


And so at first I thought the white men     / Were ghosts

one spoke my language

And said that he had spoken to my father

I did not fear them


I thought they had been

whitened by the sun     / Like bones     wandering

I thought I could / Help them

I thought they didn't


Know they were dead

2

# Purgatory: A Memoir / A Son and a Father of Sons

*I myself prefer to be left face up*
*in a ditch and for someone to go to jail*
*because of what he's done to me.*

—PRISCILLA BECKER

Ajax (within)
*Boy! Where is my child?*

—SOPHOCLES (TRANSLATED BY JOHN MOORE)

1

Most mornings, on my way to school, I would stop on the bridge over the branch of the creek that separated the school from my house and peer through the railing down at the minnows twisting in the pale current.

Some afternoons, and sometimes on the weekends, I would climb through the thick bushes behind the school—I would push, violently, sometimes knocking whole trees down, sometimes stomping on them, imagining myself hacking through a faraway jungle, and once I brought one of my grandfather's machetes with me, his only souvenirs from the army, although he hadn't fought in a war, two machetes and a pair of boots, and hacked so desperately, so gleefully then that I didn't get anywhere, but stood in one spot, hacking—and through the bamboo trees beyond the bushes, to the village of abandoned and rotting houses in the placeless clearing.

Two houses, both wooden, and both painted brown, although most of the paint had peeled away, stood in the center of the village if one were facing the village, having just emerged from the bamboo forest. To the left of the houses a narrow dirt road led away from the village. To the right of the houses stood a building that looked like a cross between a barn and a warehouse. It, too, was brown, and brown also where the paint had peeled away, exposing the wood underneath.

The village was the emptiest place I had ever seen. But the warehouse and the houses were full. The houses were full of furniture nobody had used in years, and old kitchen appliances, and shoes—I remember several pairs of shoes—and stained jeans. In the first house I walked through, the first couch I saw had been tilted on its back. It lay in a small living room, and next to it was a pair of cracked brown wingtip oxfords, and a few feet in front of it were two empty, beaten-up suitcases; otherwise, it was surrounded by old sheets of plywood and fragments of the walls. The houses stood even though they looked as if more material had been torn from the walls than could have been in the walls in the first place.

The houses and the warehouse were separated by about 100 feet of dirt, and patches of broken concrete, and thorny, low bushes, and grass. I call it a village, but there wasn't more to it than what I've just described. I call it a village because it was abandoned—the words seem to go together—and filled with trash and also things I thought people wouldn't have left behind, things that looked important to me, toys, mostly, some whole and some broken, all filthy, mostly in the warehouse. I remember the ivory-colored stuffed bear I saw near the bottom left corner of the mouth of the warehouse—the first thing I saw in the warehouse, the thing that drew me to the warehouse—best. But toys were scattered all over the floor of the warehouse, and at the back of the warehouse—I only visited the warehouse once, after I had visited the houses several times, and didn't return to the village for months afterward—I saw a door, like the front door of a house, but deep and far in darkness.

Back then—I was six or seven years old—as now, fear compelled me toward the things I feared, and so I made my way slowly—and I lost my balance a few times, slipping on stuffed animals or dolls or fire trucks or doll parts—to the door, and turned the handle, and pushed. On the other side was a small workroom with a desk—a board about the size of a door, but smaller, laid across two saw horses—a dirty chair with metal legs and brown vinyl padding on the seat and the back, and a few shelves full of paint cans. A dusty toolbox, a small lamp with a flexible neck and a metal, cup-shaped head, and a Phillips screwdriver sat on the desk. The room's single window was intact, and sunlight fell through it and across the desk, striking the head of the lamp, which glowed. I stared at the glowing lamp, terrified, feeling suddenly near, as children sometimes for imaginary reasons do, death, hoping the lamp was on.

## JIM LIMBER THE ADOPTED MULATTO SON OF JEFFERSON DAVIS MET HIS ADOPTIVE MOTHER VARINA DAVIS AT A CROSSROADS

Up north it's midnight in America
Here in America it's midnight too
Daddy Jeff says he    says it was always two
Americas and he just keeps it law
I don't know    anything about the law
Except I know what's true and isn't true
But sometimes I'll see Negroes running through
A field in the dark and not say what I saw

When white folks ask    I tell them I was happy
With momma and she didn't beat me of-
ten till the war got bad    but we was going
North and I didn't want to go the morning
Momma Varina rescued me    she whups me
Different    like what she wants from it is love

## 2

Later, months after or before, when I wake in the sharp grass, and the large, older boy, who a moment, a minute, how long was it ago had been crushing my chest against the brick pillar at the edge of my porch, and every inch of my body except for my chest had felt like it was disappearing, and alongside that feeling, the other feeling, the feeling I had been looking for, the feeling I had asked him to give me, please, after he had offered it, guessing I must want it, the feeling that my body was no longer mine, is now standing above me, and my skin burns where each blade of grass touches it, and I feel the world more particularly than I've ever felt it before, and so I hurt in a way I've never hurt before, when I wake, the first question I ask, thinking it would be like this, to return to my body, burning, is, "Am I dead?"

And the large, older boy doesn't answer me. The large, older boy doesn't help me up. It's the first time the large, older boy has visited my house during the day, and after he leaves, the large, older boy will never come back—not during the day, and not at night. I lie in the grass, not sure whether I'm supposed to stand. The corners of the large, older boy's disproportionately large mouth turn down. Then he calls me a faggot and walks away.

I was passed around the neighborhood as a child—never from adult to adult, mostly from child to child, and sometimes from child to teenager to child—not me in my body, but the rumor of me and my body, according to which I took my place in the world more surely than if I stood where the rumor went. I must have met the large, older boy who, the day we met, told me to leave my bedroom window unlocked for him later, on that circuit, but I don't remember where, or when. He was much bigger than me—a child, also, but old enough and big enough that I couldn't form a clear idea of his age, and he seemed, as all older, much bigger children seemed, somehow bigger than my father, who was, anyway, my grandfather, the man raising me who was married to the woman raising me. He might have been a teenager.

I was afraid of the large, older boy from the moment I met him—I don't remember much about the moment itself, but I remember the fear, and I remember he threatened to beat me up if I didn't leave my bedroom window unlocked for him. But I would have left it unlocked even if he hadn't threatened me. When I was a child, I was willing, even eager, to let anybody do anything they wanted to me, so long as they didn't hurt me, and so long as what they were doing looked like the things I saw people doing in my grandfather's magazines, which seemed, especially among the boys I met, common—not my grandfather's magazines in particular, but most of the neighborhood boys found similar magazines in their own homes—and in which we discovered, not images corresponding to any overwhelming desires we might have felt, but guides to the overwhelming desires encompassing us. What I remember most distinctly is not any single act, but the sensation I felt, both empty and vast, as I watched what people did to me, and what I did to them, reluctantly, but I would if they asked me to, checking to make sure it looked right, familiar. I was comfortable in that vastness, and afraid of it, and I hated it, and yearned toward it, but not toward *it*, exactly, but toward people I thought might be familiar with it, as my grandfather was, and willing to inflict it.

## JEFFERSON DAVIS THE ADOPTIVE FATHER
## OF THE MULATTO JIM LIMBER DREAMS
## OF AN UNKNOWING LOVE

*She is a slim young     Negress but I know*
*she is my Varina she is a girl*
*I saw only once     a few weeks ago*
*in town on an errand with her master*

*whom she resembled and his wife who did*
*not look at her     but commanded the air*
*immediately before her own     face*
*and the Negress three steps behind obeyed*

*she was nobody she is     Varina*
*I recognize her as she was and is*
*two women in a single body I*
*stand hidden     in a shadow in the dream*

*watching but I stood in the sun when I*

*saw her but things    are not as they were and*

*I stand hidden in a shadow    and as*

*she passes three steps behind her master*


*who had passed half a step behind his wife*

*I reach for her    and in the way of dreams*

*touching her    who was the moment before*

*a stranger I know her    and have known her*


*from the moment of her birth    and in the*

*way of dreams also she is new to me*

*as the moon is she is    both known and strange*

*I pull her    into the darkness that hides*


*me from her master and his wife and hid*

*me from her before    and there I desire*

*her as a white man desires a Negress*

*as two women in a single body*


*I draw her close to me    and as I reach*

*for her face her master's    wife calls her name*

Varina *she calls    where are you and she*

*calls with my Varina's voice she calls her*

*name    and mixes it with mine    Jefferson*

*where are you I have fallen    asleep in*

*my study    my Varina calls for me*

*as the moon calls    for the light of the sun*


*from across an unknowable blackness*

## JIM LIMBER THE ADOPTED MULATTO SON
## OF JEFFERSON DAVIS INHERITS THE KINGDOM
## OF THE NEGRO IN AMERICA

I lived with momma for a nigger's age

For seven years     since I was seven I

Ain't seen her once and now I'm almost eight

I think she must be free     momma Vari-

na she     says it don't matter who your mom-

ma was if you're a man she says *Are you*

*A man Jim look at Joe*     I look at him

But I don't see me in his eyes but two


Blue shadows that ain't black like shadows should be

I look at him and I don't see no way

For me to be a man but I see daddy

Jeff and my face is shadows in his eyes

I look at Joe     he got     daddy Jeff's face

My daddy's white     so I don't get his face

3

My grandfather—although I don't know whether he would have described himself in this way—was a white supremacist. He wouldn't have been ashamed to admit that he believed white people were superior to black people—*especially* superior to black people *in particular*—indeed, he happily—or, really, "gleefully" would probably be a better word, since white supremacists don't ever seem happy so much as gleeful—admitted to this belief many times when I was a child. But I suspect he might have thought the phrase "white supremacist" was too fancy for him. He had been, as a child, the younger brother of a much larger boy, and, along with his older brother Thomas, and his younger brother, Raymond—who grew up to become a landlord, who would eventually be shot through the neck by a tenant he had evicted a few days before, and would die in a soft-top convertible, blood spraying from his neck, his head rolling slightly from side to side on his shoulder as he pointed toward a narrow gap between two dumpsters, wordlessly urging his wife, who was already crawling away from the car, to safety—as a child, had lived in poverty, in the wake of the Dust Bowl, in Shawnee, Oklahoma. Because of and despite this, he hated "white trash" almost as much—although the hate was a different kind of hate, a sad duty—as he hated blacks, my father especially.

I tracked my father down when I was 16—by then, my grandparents had divorced and I was living with my grandmother in Salem, Oregon, where I had lived with my father when I was a baby—and it was then that I learned my grandparents had taken me from him when I was three, and not, as they had so often told me, when I was 18 months old. And of all the lies I was told as a child, this lie has been the hardest lie to shake—it won't, in fact, not yet, anyway, be shaken. When I think about it now, which isn't often, but I do, being taken, I imagine myself as both 18 months and three years old, and the scene in which I am disappeared plays out twice; I see the two versions simultaneously. In one version, I'm naked except for a diaper, splashing in a dirty puddle at the end of my driveway in Round Rock as my grandmother tends to the row of flowers between her new house and her new lawn, her back to her new child; in the other version, I'm fully clothed, wearing a half maroon, half gray T-shirt, the two colors separated by a white stripe about a half-inch thick—maroon above, gray below—and bell-bottom jeans, and riding a big wheel my father has just given me, when my grandmother lifts me from the big wheel to put me in the back seat of my grandparents' big, white Dodge 4-door, and as she carries me to the car I cry out, and reach back for the big wheel. I'm afraid I will lose it forever, but then I lose it forever.

My grandparents took me to Round Rock. They told my mother she would never see me again if she told my father where I was. The first thing my grandfather did—that was the way my grandmother always told the story—the first thing he did after we moved into our new house was throw me into a wall, the living room wall, the stretch of wall, maybe four feet wide—in a few years he would hang a painting of a Native American crouching to touch the still surface of a lake, which he later replaced with a self-portrait, there—next to the big, sliding glass door that opened to the back yard, which I loved but can't really remember anymore, not anything good about it, but I remember the time the neighborhood flooded and the septic tank burst or maybe just overflowed, but it seemed like it must have been overflowing for years because the whole yard, and it was a big yard, was covered with about an inch or so of watery sewage, the grass was swimming in it, but also the grass was still, but also the grass was drowned.

The minnows clustered there, on the left side of the bridge if one were facing the school, if one had stopped on the way to the school. There the creek seemed to slow down a little before it filtered through the three small tunnels underneath the bridge. On the other side of the bridge, the creek emptied into a shallow pond—about a foot to two feet deep, and about 30 feet wide by 80 feet long—but the pond water was too dirty to see anything in it. The minnows might have passed through the tunnels into the dirty, dark pond—every morning, I might have been seeing new minnows swirling in the bright shallows—or they might have known to fight hardest there, at the mouths of the tunnels, where the water was still clear, against the darkness the element they lived in pushed and pulled them toward.

JEFFERSON DAVIS THE ADOPTIVE FATHER
OF THE MULATTO JIM LIMBER DREAMS
THE FUTURE OF THE AMERICAN ENTERTAINMENT
INDUSTRY AS HE DREAMS HE IS ARGUING
HIS CAUSE IN WASHINGTON D.C.

*The wheel of history turns in the gut*

*of the white man     but the Negro is strapped*

*to the wheel     and broken by the turning*

*and nearly liquefied by the turning*


*and the white man sickens     to him who says*

*we do not pay for the life we enjoy*

*I say we pay with our sickness     I say*

*our enjoyment is not what you suppose*


*but it is     instead a life of worry*

*and disappointed love     to him I say*

*yes     we love our Negroes and with a great*

*love Yankees cannot know and would not want*

*to know if they could     and to those who would*

*free the Negro I     say look to your guts*


*you fatten on the people you would free*

## JIM LIMBER THE ADOPTED MULATTO SON OF JEFFERSON DAVIS WAS ANOTHER CHILD FIRST

They put me in a dead boy's clothes dead Joseph

Except he wasn't dead at first they put

Me in his clothes dead Joseph's    after Joseph

Died and I used to call him Joe    they put

Me in Joe's clothes at first before he died

Joe wasn't five yet when I met him    I

Was seven    I was seven when he died

Still but a whole year bigger then but I

Wore his clothes still and the whole year I lived with

Momma Varina    and with daddy Jeff

I never lived so good as when I lived with

Them and especially it was daddy Jeff

Who kept me fed and wearing those nice clothes

Until they fit as tight as bandages

## JIM LIMBER THE ADOPTED MULATTO SON OF JEFFERSON DAVIS CANNOT DEPEND UPON POLITICAL OR ECONOMIC POWER TO BE THE WELLSPRING OF HIS FREEDOM

I ask myself what     man would daddy Jeff

Be if he weren't the president I ask

Myself because I do not know myself

And I can't ask     anyone else I think

He would be president of something small-

er than America     like Richmond or

Even just the house I     reckon even then all

The Negroes in the county would admire

Him and he would be president of the Ne-

groes     I would vote for him     sometimes he lets

Me vote and he says *Vote     as Joe if he*

*Could vote would vote* I vote we eat dessert

First and I run to tell the kitchen     like I'm

A president     and since     I eat in the kitchen

4

The house immediately to the right of my house if one were facing my house, having just walked home, bleeding, from a fight on the playground at the school across the street, was a rental. My grandparents often pointed this out to me as a warning. And I understood they meant that the families who lived in the house, never for longer than a year, had less money than my family did. And I treated the house and its backyard like they were empty even when they weren't.

Usually, the families who lived in the house immediately to the right of mine didn't have pets. But once, a family with a dog lived there, a small dog, it seemed small to me even when I was small, but it was probably about half my size. I used to play with the dog beneath the fence that separated our yards. I had dug a hole between our yards, or the dog had, and I would stick my hand under the fence and throw things for the dog to fetch. This was the first dog I ever tortured, and it might have been the last—I can't recall torturing another dog after it, but my cats before, and a small bird after—and I stopped harming animals altogether when I was about eight or nine years old, and this, the dog I'm remembering, torturing it, must have happened when I was six or seven. One day, for no reason, I don't think I had a reason, the dog had never hurt me, I grabbed a length of lead pipe, and called the dog to the hole, and when it stuck its nose into the hole, I smashed the end of it with the pipe. This is what I remember most clearly about the dog, this and not the dog and I playing—smashing the dog's nose again and again with the pipe, eventually the end of the pipe, which was about two inches in diameter, jamming it at the dog's nose, and the blood, the dog snarling, its teeth bared, biting the hole.

## JIM LIMBER THE ADOPTED MULATTO SON OF JEFFERSON DAVIS CANNOT AFFORD TO MAKE DEMANDS OF LOVE

Momma Varina feels for Negroes daddy

Jeff says she feels for Negroes more than what

She should but he don't tell her what she should be

Feeling    for Negroes he's the president

And what's more daddy    Jeff and if he want-

ed to he could    instead he talks to me

A lot of the time he talks to me about

Things he don't talk he    says to nobody

About he says    it's something like a Ne-

gro cannot listen    like the folks he owes

A duty to    and that's a great relief

I know he's scared sometimes    but he don't show

It much to nobody    else    that's how I know he

Loves me    because he don't mind what he shows me

## JEFFERSON DAVIS THE ADOPTIVE FATHER OF THE MULATTO JIM LIMBER DREAMS THE FREEDOM OF THE NEGRO WILL ONE DAY BE HIS FREEDOM

*I see the declaration passing from*
*hand to hand from Washington to Richmond*
*from horse to horse    from rider to rider*
*one galloping furiously until*

*his horse falls dead at the hooves of the next*
*most trotting    some walking    one paused and let*
*his fat horse nibble at grass for an hour*
*while he chatted with a schoolgirl in Maine*

*the declaration winds through every state*
*and territory    answering the cries*
*of the soil for the blood of native sons*
*now mixed with the soil of distant places*

not with each drop     disentangled and brought
home     but with news of my full and uncon-
ditional pardon     which is no answer
and the soil of every state and every

territory     after it has been kicked
or scooped     into the air it     doesn't fall
but floats behind the rider     and much of
the soil beneath it rises to meet it

and it's a cresting wake of dirt and mud
follows the instrument of my freedom
it floats     about six feet above the ground
not as an unbroken stream     but instead

every few yards     there is a small gap
and each     segment of dirt     slowly resolves
into a human shape     from the head down
so that at first clumps of dirt seem to be

falling     but as they fall they spread apart
and branch into arms     then a chest     then legs
then feet     which finally touch the pitted earth
and these dark men march behind     the pardon

neither for any reason    faster nor

slower ever but ever marching at

a mourner's pace    but I see the last    rid-

er is Lincoln    and his horse floats    and breeds


no men    though they come    but they come so slow-

ly    through ruined Virginia    the pardon

reaches me days before the men    who will

kill me    and I begin to plan my life

## JIM LIMBER THE ADOPTED MULATTO SON OF
## JEFFERSON DAVIS CONSIDERS HIS PLACE IN HISTORY

Mostly I hear him     daddy Jeff before

I see him he     talks to himself     real loud when

He walks I hear him mostly     anywhere

In the house even     when I'm in the yard and


Momma Varina says a gentleman

Announces his     presence with his     demeanor

I don't know what that means I think it means

She wants him just to hush sometimes     I seen her


Crying and slap him once and the next day

The Yankees marched on Petersburg and that

Was yesterday     today     he pulls me a-


side and he says he don't know where they'll take me

That scared me good     but he     just floats off     talking

Just like a ghost     just like I ain't his ghost

## 5

About a year later—on my birthday, actually, the last day of summer—
I rode my bike down the gravel road to the left of my school—a road
I had often taken to soccer practice—farther than ever before, think-
ing it might eventually intersect with the dirt road that led away from
the village, all the way until it curved sharply into darkness, where the
road met a forest that had risen just past the soccer fields and baseball
diamonds, or almost all the way, really, until about 70 feet before the
curve, and there, by the side of the road, I laid my bike down and
stepped toward the forest.

The forest was thick, and dark, and mostly, I think, oak, and some cedar trees. I don't know for sure why I stopped where I stopped, but I think I might have noticed, glancing at the forest as I headed toward the curve I probably wouldn't have ridden past even if I had reached it, the shadowy, almost overgrown path into the forest, and stopped to investigate it. Back then, the forests near my house were littered with abandoned treehouses—well, most of the treehouses were just boards wedged between branches and trunks so as to create perches, but a few had walls and even roofs, and all were invisible unless one stood fairly close to them. In one of the better treehouses, in a forest not far from the forest I had just entered, I had discovered, just the previous Saturday, half a pack of cigarettes and a few old copies of *Hustler*. Probably, I entered this forest looking for the same treehouse—or, rather, hoping the treehouse with the walls, and the cigarettes, and the pornography would be repeated in this forest, like an outpost station stocked with standard rations. At first, as I followed the path, I saw nothing but tall trees and thick foliage. But soon I noticed a wrought-iron fence to my right, itself almost disappeared by foliage, and beyond it I saw graves.

The cemetery looked like it hadn't been visited or maintained in years. Most of the 20 or so stones were dark, almost black, almost illegible, and stood only a few feet tall—there were no monuments, and no statutes. But nearest to the gate, to the left of the gate if one were facing the gate, sweaty from pedaling, but chilly, also, already, shivering in the unusually strong wind that day, lay a large, flat stone, which at first I thought had fallen. I had walked in a counterclockwise circle around the perimeter of the cemetery, just inside the fence, and so I had seen this stone last, and when I stopped and stared down at it, I realized it hadn't fallen—it seemed, instead, to be covering a grave. I can't remember the inscription exactly, but I do remember I had to bend close to the stone to read it. The stone memorialized 18 children who had died when a nearby orphanage burned to the ground 70 years before. It didn't seem possible to me even then, when I was a small child and most things seemed possible, that the stone marked a mass grave, that the children had all been buried in the same spot, but I couldn't imagine they were anywhere else. What families would have claimed them? And I felt sure that if I moved the stone and peered into the hole, I would see the orphans in the fire still, motionless, some prone, some on all fours, some kneeling, hunched, and blackened, and the orphanage intact still, burning, and the whole world of wrecked, and burned, and abandoned things, each trapped in the moment of its destruction, each thing preserved, both dead and outside of death, not in Hell, but in the one fire everywhere, after which there is no suffering, and so from which there is no relief.

# 3

## Banjo Yes Receives a
## Lifetime Achievement Award

I ain't no never had to never done

No acting not like some of these white boys / Nothing

you'll find in books

y'all listen close / Now    and I'll tell you how I got my name


I worked on    as a young man on a lot

What do you think I did I cleaned I fetched

Shit and more shit shit both ways shit and took

And kept it too yes    and whenever I thought


A white boy might be calling me hell    yes    / I answered

one    morning and I'm just cross-

ing from one thing to the next I hear a shout

*Banjo* and so    I lift my head but not


Too high that ain't my name and I say *Yes*

Back loud but    real polite    and this white boy

I never seen before and he's away

Over the other side of the lot but each

Of the white boys there he had a different

Important way of standing and no I

Ain't seen this boy before he had his fists

Jammed in his hips like all of them but he


Leaned heavy on his left leg like he was

Limping standing still     I run quick o-

ver to him I say *Yes sir* tells me to

Bend down and wipe this     is the truth it was


A spot of bird shit from his shoe

this ain't     / No kind of story where the nigger says

*No* I bent down and cleaned his shoe

I can't     / From down there see the look on the man's face


From down there at his feet but just as I

Get started     and I think he must have been

Smiling he says *Is your name Banjo* I

Say *No sir my name's Bill* and he     says *Ban-*


*jo suits you better     Banjo Yes     and when*

*I talk to you that's who you're gonna be*

And I say *Yes sir sir your shoe is clean*

Now listen     that boy he was nobody

In fact I never saw that boy again

But that name stuck to me

and when you see     / A white boy talking on the screen     that's him

And when you see me smiling back that's me

# Banjo Yes Recalls His First Movies

Most of the time I spent
In the beginning most of the time between

Scenes I spent chasing after their
filth in my mind     / They had me playing

Servants and when the cameras stopped I kept on cleaning
What was it like

The thing about white folks     back then was     / They was what was
What it was     what     they white folks did was you was like

A mind in something in a body but
that body wasn't yours

I'll tell you what it was like it was
That body was

A second mind     / Talking
your body was a voice like you was talking to yourself

Telling you do    like you supposed to do white
folks the way they talk about

Their cars    their houses    niggers    they talk like
Owning a thing a man is something they / Do with their hands

and niggers    we're
we    got to be    / Free if we ain't in chains

Well    back when I was starting out
the only talking I could do on screen was talking

chains around myself    / And who
was it who    / Paid me to talk

White folks stay clean
'cause how they own you is they own    your options

You can be free
Or you can live

# Banjo Yes Talks About
# His First White Wife

Thing is she hated her

Father    her mother and her brothers    loved

Her cousin but he stopped

Coming around    / After she married me no letters said

He didn't have a phone

So every Christmas every birthday every

Goddamn    / Armistice Day I sent that boy a phone

She didn't know I did that    but I made sure he knew it was me

I sent    / The same note every time *Don't*

*Worry I got a white boy here he answers our*

*Calls*    see    he wanted that and didn't want it

A nigger    can surround himself with whiteness

But it becomes a wall between him / And whiteness

and he wants and doesn't want it

# Banjo Yes Plucks an Apple from a Tree in a Park

FOR TAMIR RICE

I hold an apple in my hand on set

It is     or ain't    an apple ain't a real

Apple depending on     am I in the shot

Or am I watching with the crew     a real


Apple don't taste no sweeter than a movie

Apple it ain't    crisper    but it's some better

A nigger eats an apple in a movie

It ain't no apple it's a big     fat     water-


melon man it's fried chicken it's all that

Bullshit    a nigger eats but he ain't eating

No nigger in no movie ever got

Hungry and ate and it was just him eating

No nigger tells the story of himself

Man even if I *hate* a nigger what-

ever he does    *I* do    I ask myself

Before I do    anything it don't mat-


ter what it is *Who's    watching me*    and *What*

*They gonna think they see*    I waste my mind

Trying to read white folks' minds    I'll tell you what

An apple is    it's death    it's my child dead

# Banjo Yes Talks About Motivation

The difference was they had names like a name

a boy    / Might think a grown man wants    / The white boys

did the actors names like Rex    and Duke    / We niggers

had names like a name a boy might get for

Some stupid shit

He did once when he wasn't thinking when he did it

Like    they would call a nigger Hambone Jones

Because a white boy spotted him    sucking on a ham bone

Probably    thinking about his woman

and he's hungry and he's poor

They named you for a thing

your hunger made you do

And what could you say back

You're not    a man and you're a poor man


What won't you do

## Banjo Yes Asks a Journalist

I didn't marry none of them white women

Because I was a    / What did you say    *a free black man*

Shit man if I had been a free black man

I would have married a girl from back home


That's what you think it is

Freedom you don't you you think it's

Making decisions other folks won't like

Listen    I do a thing to piss a white man off


I'm bound to that man's will    hell

I'm bound to that man's *pleasure*

He got me on a level where he doesn't even have to think

And all I do is think about him


tell me    when have I been free

Boy write this down    I'm asking

when have you not had to say / Something about white folks to say

Something about me

4

# (hope)(lessness)

*And when your goal is nearest*
*The end for others sought,*
*Watch sloth and heathen Folly*
*Bring all your hopes to nought.*
—RUDYARD KIPLING

The keeper keeps me     / He tells me

Because he has no hope

I have become an

Expression     of his hopelessness // My kind

out-breeds his kind

he says     / And I have lived

With the keeper long enough to know

He thinks that means // Eventually

my kind

Will murder him and everyone he loves

and live in / His house

And eat his bread

He fears he can't defend

His house     his bread he

Has put his faith in things

That can't be loyal in return


And also all his hope is gone

Because     he tells me

he has kept me for so long

How could he     / Free me


And not fear I / Would seek revenge     / He says

he keeps me here

because he would if he were

Me seek revenge


He is a strange

Man he will not acknowledge

my humanity     in-

sofar as it is mine     / But will


Ascribe his traits to me

in all     / Their human / Complexity

it even

pleases him to do so

I tell him // He is hopeful      / He doesn't fear me

Because I'm different from him

but because he hopes

I will become him

## Sunlight

I've been in a white man's
Skin in my body
and I have returned to tell you

Never in my life I
Ever felt more afraid
Nor ever in my life

So capable    so strong
Until I wasn't I    had been a colored
woman all my life

as pale
As any colored woman
Born from a white man's property

And I felt pale inside
But never white inside    or / Inside
I felt    / Colored inside but colored white

Like I    was truly white

The color white and

The master and his family


Were clear as glass / The clear

bright white not white of

Sunlight on glass


That's what they meant when they said *white*

I / Didn't feel white like that

Inside


I worked in the house the mistress

wasn't bad or good to me

I spent my childhood with her children


but    / About when I turned thirteen

Her sons one

thirteen and the other ten


Began to look too long at me

The older for himself    the younger for the older

The mistress noticed

and soon I was sent

into the fields     / Not I don't think

To keep us separate


but to keep the boys from doing

In the house what they wanted

To do to me in the house


I think it's white folks what they want

It isn't really or it isn't just

to / Not see the wrong


They want to not see

It and they want to know

It's happening where it belongs


I spent four years in the fields

It was worse than you might care to think it was

But then one     day it was a / Hot day I saw the strangest


thing I caught a glimpse of my / Face

in still water in a bowl I saw the

Older boy's face I almost     jumped

Right then I knew     / I could be free

Three weeks / Later I took     some of the older boy's

clothes and some money from the house and


I walked away

In the night I walked away and in the morning

I bought a ticket north


and / Nobody looked at me except to nod

I rode the train with slaves and their

Masters the slaves looked


Down at their feet

I caught myself

Looking down once or twice their masters I


Don't know what they were looking at

Except I think I saw

It in a sunbeam as the sunbeam


lit the window by my head

The dust in the air

the lint

I know it was lint

but it looked like worms

flying in the light

## Jim Limber the Adopted Mulatto Son of Jefferson Davis Visits His Adoptive Parents After the War

The man said I could see them if I wanted

He said    America would never be

A place where we could    love each other not at

Least in my lifetime    but the dead don't see


No important differences    between the Ne-

gro and the White the dead    don't see no bad

In folks if what bad they done they ain't free-

ly chose to do the dead don't see    no good


In folks if what good they done they ain't    hoped

To do and the man    he said    part of momma

Varina part of daddy    Jeff alread-

y    was burning in Hell I ought to join them


He said    we might see good    from seeing each other

Tortured    we might finally see each other

## Asked About *The Banjo Man* and Its Sequels Banjo Yes Tells a Journalist Something About Himself

My aunt my momma's sister

She had a real good

piano had it right

in her front room there

She lived just up the street I

used to    when I was a boy / I used to

hide in her

Bushes when she was giving lessons just

To hear her play

I don't know why I hid

She loved Chopin and all of them

She and my momma had some differences between them

well      / One afternoon I walk

over to her house

Because I know she has a lesson coming


But when I get there      her front      door it's wide

Open and I don't hear no music just a few

Bad notes      but not


like how a child plays bad

I sit in the bushes anyway      just wait-

ing for a while      but / After a while


the house gets      quiet so

I peek through the window

And then I see it her      front room it's all tore      up / Some


fool I guess

Robbed her      busted her      / Things up busted her

piano too      / Just to be mean I guess my


Aunt she's just sitting on the bench just

staring

but she must have heard me      / Because she

turns    and smiles and she

starts to stand up she

leans forward she takes her    / Hands    they was resting


on the keyboard from the keyboard

And grips the front edge of the bench

I watch her hands    but at the same time I see


every part of her and every    part of her

Looks bigger like I'm focused on it

Like if you made a picture of a woman / From cut up pictures


from a magazine

And nothing fits together

but it's her but I don't recognize her


And shit man I don't know


what it was but I    never will forget it shit my heart

Starts pounding and

I    / All of a sudden I can't    breathe and I

Run I run home I run so hard I throw up

Soon as I shut     the front door right there / Got my ass

whipped for that


But not for running but for throwing up

I told my momma

everything and all she did was shake her head


And you know     *Mmm mmm mmm* and *What*

*A shame* and she went back to what she had been

Doing in the kitchen


and I followed her

And I sat down and waited / Like I was waiting

For supper     and we didn't talk about my aunt no more


Anyway     no     I never learned to play no banjo

no     in the movies I just

Wiggled my fingers


and they laid the music over me

## Still When I Picture It the Face of God Is a White Man's Face

Before it disappears

on the sand his long white     beard before it disappears

The face of the man

in the waves I ask her does she see it ask her does

The old man in the waves     as the waves crest she see it does

she see the old man his

White     his face crumbling face it looks

as old as he's as old as

The ocean looks

and for a moment almost looks

His face like it's     all the way him

As never such old skin

looks my / Daughter age four

She thinks it might he might be real she shouts *Hello*

And after there's no answer answers *No*

# Acknowledgments

Thanks to Dan Chaon, Gabriel Fried, Jorie Graham, Garth Greenwell, Derek Gromadzki, Melissa McCrae, Wesley Rothman, Suzanna Tamminen, and G. C. Waldrep for their advice, counsel, presence, and patience. And thanks to the editors and staffs of the following journals, in which earlier versions of these poems first appeared:

*Bear Review*: "Jefferson Davis the Adoptive Father of the Mulatto Jim Limber Dreams the Future of the American Entertainment Industry as He Dreams He Is Arguing His Cause in Washington D.C." and "Jim Limber the Adopted Mulatto Son of Jefferson Davis Cannot Afford to Make Demands of Love"

*Conduit*: "Banjo Yes Asks a Journalist" and "Banjo Yes Talks About Motivation"

*Gulf Coast*: "His God" and "Panopticon"

*Handsome*: "What Do You Know About Shame"

*Horsethief*: "Jim Limber the Adopted Mulatto Son of Jefferson Davis Cannot Depend Upon Political or Economic Power to Be the Wellspring of His Freedom" and "Jim Limber the Adopted Mulatto Son of Jefferson Davis Inherits the Kingdom of the Negro in America"

*Lit Hub*: "(hope)(lessness)"

*Missouri Review*: "Jim Limber the Adoptive Mulatto Son of Jefferson Davis Met His Adoptive Mother Varina Davis at a Crossroads"

*Omniverse*: "In the Language," "Privacy," and "Privacy 2"

*Pinwheel*: "Banjo Yes Receives a Lifetime Achievement Award" and "Banjo Yes Talks About His First White Wife"

*Poetry*: "Jim Limber the Adopted Mulatto Son of Jefferson Davis Was Another Child First" and "Still When I Picture It the Face of God Is a White Man's Face"

*The Rumpus*: "Banjo Yes Plucks and Apple from a Tree in a Park"

*The Spectacle*: "Banjo Yes Recalls His First Movies"

*West Branch Wired*: "Jim Limber the Adoptive Mulatto Son of Jefferson Davis Considers His Place in History" and "Jefferson Davis the Adoptive Father of the Mulatto Jim Limber Dreams of an Unknowing Love"

Parts of "Purgatory: A Memoir" appeared in an e-chapbook called *30 Paragraphs*, published by Essay Press.

"Jim Limber the Adopted Mulatto Son of Jefferson Davis Visits His Adoptive Parents After the War" was originally published as part of the Academy of American Poets' Poem-A-Day project.

"His God" was republished by *Poetry Daily*.

"Sunlight" was originally published as part of the PEN American Center's Poetry Series.

"Still When I Picture It the Face of God Is a White Man's Face" was republished in *Pushcart Prize XLI: Best of the Small Presses*.

**Shane McCrae** teaches at Oberlin College and Spalding University. He is the recipient of a Whiting Writers' Award and a National Endowments for the Arts Fellowship. He is the author of many volumes of poetry, including *The Animal Too Big to Kill* (Persea Books, 2015); *Forgiveness Forgiveness* (Factory Hollow Press, 2014); and *Blood* (Noemi Press, 2013).